IMAGES
of America

CHESAPEAKE BAY
SHIPWRECKS

The once-proud *District of Columbia*, built in 1925, operated on the Chesapeake Bay until the early 1960s, when—renamed *Provincetown*—she became a summer cruise ferry between Boston and Provincetown, Massachusetts. New owners brought her back to Baltimore to be converted into a restaurant-bar in New Jersey. But the dream never panned out. At Baltimore's Pratt Street Pier 3, she was destroyed by fire on June 5, 1969. Towed to Curtis Bay, south of Baltimore's Inner Harbor and a notorious refuge for abandoned and derelict vessels, she deteriorated until finally slipping under the water in 1971. (Courtesy of Jack Shaum.)

ON THE COVER: The *State of Virginia* joined the Old Bay Line in 1923 as an overnight service primarily between Baltimore and Norfolk, Virginia. On the evening of July 14, 1936, returning to Baltimore after a two-day excursion with some 235 raucous conventioneers of the Maryland Automobile Trade Association and Maryland governor Henry W. Nice onboard, she collided with the freighter *Golden Harvest* at the mouth of the Patapsco River. Miraculously, no one was badly injured, but the vessels remained locked and drifted aground. (With permission from the *Baltimore Sun*.)

IMAGES
of America

CHESAPEAKE BAY SHIPWRECKS

William B. Cogar

ARCADIA
PUBLISHING

Published by Arcadia Publishing
Charleston, South Carolina

Printed in the United States of America

Library of Congress Control Number: 2019935929

For all general information, please contact Arcadia Publishing:
Telephone 843-853-2070
Fax 843-853-0044
E-mail sales@arcadiapublishing.com
For customer service and orders:
Toll-Free 1-888-313-2665

Visit us on the Internet at www.arcadiapublishing.com

*Dedicated to all those who love and appreciate the Chesapeake Bay, its
beauty, and its history. May shipwrecks become a thing of the past.*

CONTENTS

ACKNOWLEDGMENTS

The photographic and material cultural history of the beautiful Chesapeake Bay is fortunately maintained and shared by a host of very talented, caring, and generous individuals, all of whom receive my most sincere thanks and appreciation. Chief among them are those at two of the finest maritime museums on the Bay. At The Mariners' Museum and Park in Newport News, Virginia, I cannot thank enough Marc Marsocci, director of digital services; Jeanne Willoz-Egnor, director of collections management; Sarah Puckitt, curator of photography; Bill Barker, archivist; and Lisa Williams, of digital services. Similarly, the Chesapeake Bay Maritime Museum in St. Michael's, Maryland, has an incredible collection overseen by Pete Lesher, chief curator, and Jenifer Dolde, collections manager.

Others who provided invaluable help in this project include Astrid Drew, archivist at the Steamship Historical Society of America in Warwick, Rhode Island; Joseph Judge, curator at the Hampton Roads Naval Museum in Norfolk, Virginia; Dr. Susan Langley, state underwater archaeologist for the Maryland Historic Trust in Annapolis, Maryland; Janet Ridgley of the Reedville Fisherman's Museum in Reedville, Virginia; Dave Colamaria, director of the Photography Division at the Naval History and Heritage Command at the Washington, DC, Navy Yard; Tracie Logan, senior curator at the US Naval Academy Museum in Annapolis, Maryland; and Nora L. Chinloe, archivist of the US Coast Guard Historian's Office in Washington, DC. All were so very helpful.

My thanks also go out to Tim Thomas of the Baltimore Sun Media Group; Skip Lewis of Gloucester, Virginia; Gary Crawford of Tilghman Island, Maryland; Mike Smolek; Patricia McGee of the Kent County News, and Dave Anderson of David Anderson Photography. Caitrin Cunningham, senior title manager at Arcadia Publishing, has had the patience of Job. As is so often the case, several people deserve special mention. The first is my good friend Jack Shaum, an author on Chesapeake Bay steamboats, who provided me with many valuable suggestions. Finally, no work on the Chesapeake Bay is complete without first consulting the works of historian and underwater archaeologist Donald Shomette.

INTRODUCTION

Those who reside in and around the Chesapeake Bay know what a very beautiful place it is. Whether watching the stunning sunrises and sunsets, sailing its waters for recreational purposes, or earning a living by its bounty, the Chesapeake Bay is and will remain a very special place for them. In 2017, an estimated 18.2 million Americans live in the Chesapeake Bay region, many attracted by the economic opportunities and quality of life that the region provides.

Being some 200 miles from north to south, it is this nation's largest estuary, occupying 64,299 square miles. It is fed by over 150 rivers and streams coming from six states: New York, Pennsylvania, Delaware, Maryland, Virginia, and West Virginia, plus Washington, DC. The largest of the rivers feeding it are famous in and of themselves—the Susquehanna, Potomac, Patapsco, Chester, Choptank, Patuxent, Nanticoke, Rappahannock, York, James, and Elizabeth.

Not surprisingly, the Chesapeake Bay has been one of this country's major waterways from the early 17th century, when Europeans first settled here. With large port cities like Norfolk, Newport News, Baltimore, and Washington, DC, the Bay is a link—economically and strategically—in the Intracoastal Waterway of the Eastern Seaboard. It is a very busy shipping channel for commercial vessels of all types, be they small shallops plying the many rivers or huge container vessels taking diverse cargoes up and down the estuary, out into the Atlantic, or north through the Chesapeake and Delaware Canal to the ports of Wilmington, Philadelphia, and beyond.

Over roughly a century following 1850, the Chesapeake Bay was a major thoroughfare for passengers, connecting the various towns and cities on it or on many of its tributaries. As such, when one of these vessels met misfortune and wrecked, it was a dramatic event; if there was human loss, it made these wrecks even more terrible.

With the help of the scholarship of historian and underwater archaeologist Donald G. Shomette, designer Robert E. Pratt published an extraordinary map through the National Geographic Society in 2010 that shows the locations of shipwrecks around the Delmarva Peninsula. It is not an exaggeration to say that the remains of at least 2,000 wrecked vessels are listed in the Chesapeake Bay and its tributaries.

What follows here is an attempt, using the limited imagery that exists—for of course there were rarely photographers or artists around—to capture the actual events of shipwrecks. This book will hopefully show that despite its beautiful and peaceful nature, the Chesapeake Bay has had its share of tragic shipwrecks and loss of life.

A superb, albeit sad, example shows what fires do to steamboats, whose superstructures were made primarily of wood. This is what was left of the three-decker steamer *City of Baltimore* when an explosion occurred on July 29, 1937, shortly after leaving Baltimore for Norfolk with about 150 people onboard. What followed was a devastating fire that killed two and destroyed the steamer. (Courtesy of The Mariners' Museum and Park.)

One

EXPLOSIONS AND FIRES

No matter where in the world and at what time in history, nothing is more frightening to a sailor than fire. Even with the vast improvements in more modern times in methods of fire prevention and fighting, explosions and fires remain the greatest hazards to seafarers. It is no surprise then that these remain major causes of shipwrecks. The advent of steam power ushered in many improvements for the transport of passengers and cargo, but it also increased the risk of fire and explosions, proven sadly true in the earliest days of steam vessels on the Chesapeake Bay.

With the exception of perhaps very short journeys, since humans have taken to the sea, fire was used on all oared or sailing vessels for cooking, softening pitch and tar, warmth, or other uses. But using fire naturally presented a huge danger. A single spark or an overturned cooking pot could easily ignite the flammable pitch and tar and cause a rapidly expanding conflagration. It is not surprising that fire was turned in favor of some sailors in times of war as early as the seventh century. Whether it was the carelessness of a sailor or a rough sea that caused an open flame to be spilled, fire was indeed a frightening fact in the sailor's life.

But the advent of iron and the revolutionary use of steam for the propulsion of ships in the early 19th century increased the risk of fire. To produce the steam required to propel the paddles on early steamboats, boilers were needed, and this meant that fire was a constant fact deep in the hull of a ship. Explosions caused by faulty equipment or by human error would become an increasing fact as steam machinery was used more and more. As the Chesapeake Bay increasingly became the economic lifeline for the transportation of both freight and passengers, the number of steamboats increased. Subsequently, and tragically, there would be some horrific examples of shipwrecks caused by fire and explosions.

On April 14, 1842, the *Medora*, the first steamboat built for the fledgling Baltimore Steam Packet Company, was completed and about to be turned over to the company. A couple hundred officials, guests, and onlookers mingled on the steamer and the dock celebrating the newest ship for the run between Baltimore and Norfolk. At about 3:30 p.m., with her paddlewheels beginning to turn, the boat's boiler exploded violently. The *Medora's* forward section was destroyed, and she immediately sank at the dock. Some 26 were killed with another 38 badly injured. The dead included the packet company's president and general agent, as well as the ship's captain. (Courtesy of the Chesapeake Bay Maritime Museum.)

Despite this horrible beginning, the *Medora* was raised and repaired, and with the new name of *Herald*, she remained on the Baltimore-Norfolk run until after the Civil War. She then became a tug on the Hudson River until abandoned in 1885. (Courtesy of The Mariners' Museum and Park.)

On November 11, 1864, the gunboat USS *Tulip* exploded in the Potomac River, killing 47. This memorial at St. Inigoes, in St. Mary's County, Maryland, at the mouth of the Potomac, was dedicated to those who died. (Author's collection.)

No image of the USS *Tulip* exists; this is her sister ship, the USS *Fuschia*. The *Tulip* was built in New York in 1862 for service in China; the Navy purchased her in June 1863, modified her to a gunboat of 240 tons with two 15-inch boilers, and detached her to the Potomac River Flotilla with orders to secure Union communications and disrupt those of the Confederacy on the Chesapeake Bay, the Potomac River, and its tributaries. (Courtesy of the Naval History and Heritage Command, Photo Archives.)

The *Tulip* was ordered to the Washington Navy Yard to get a malfunctioning boiler repaired. In his haste to get to the yard when he left his base on St. Inigoes Creek on November 11, 1864, Capt. William H. Smith ignored orders not to use the defective boiler. Off Ragged Point, Virginia, a couple of hours later, the faulty boiler exploded, and the gunboat quickly sank, killing 47 of the 57 crewmen, including Captain Smith. (Courtesy of Historical Maryland Markers.)

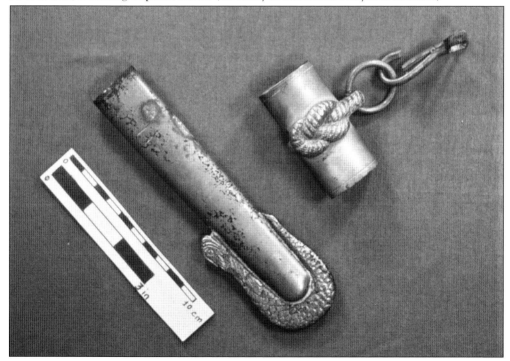

The remains of the *Tulip* were discovered in May 1994 under the authority of the Maryland Maritime Archaeology Program. Over a thousand artifacts—like these pieces of an officer's sword—having been recovered and are now part of the Naval History and Heritage Command at the Washington Navy Yard. The site sadly continues to see relic hunters. It has been nominated for listing in the National Register of Historic Places. (Courtesy of the Maryland Historical Trust, Bruce Thompson.)

The SS *Alum Chine*, built in 1905 in Glasgow, Scotland, was a small cargo steamer of 1,767 tons. She arrived in Baltimore to load about 340 tons of dynamite for use in building the Panama Canal. Anchored in the Patapsco River near the entrance to Baltimore Harbor, the ship exploded on the morning of March 7, 1913, killing over 30 and injuring more than 60. The blast was so terrific that the shockwave was felt as far away as Philadelphia and Atlantic City, New Jersey. Pieces of the ship weighing many pounds landed over three miles away. Survivors told conflicting stories, but the cause was likely spontaneous combustion in the coal bunkers. Some safety measures were implemented owing to the disaster—namely, ships loading dynamite had to do so at a greater distance from the port, and any company carrying large quantities of dynamite had to notify city authorities. (Photograph by Alfred Waldeck, *Baltimore Sun*; courtesy of the Chesapeake Bay Maritime Museum.)

Despite improvements in safety equipment and procedures, modern-day ships are still vulnerable to fires and explosions. The SS *Amerika*, launched in 1905 for Germany's Hamburg America Line, took thousands of passengers across the North Atlantic. But with the outbreak of World War I in 1914 and to prevent seizure by the British, the *Amerika* docked at neutral Boston. She remained there until April 1917, when, with the United States' entry into the war, she was seized by the US Shipping Board. (Courtesy of the Naval History and Heritage Command, Photo Archives.)

Transferred to the US Navy as a troop transport, her name was anglicized to the SS *America*. She is shown here returning to New York with US troops in August 1919. Throughout World War I, the SS *America* transported some 40,000 troops to France and over 51,000 home from Europe. (Courtesy of the Naval History and Heritage Command, Photo Archives.)

The *America* was plagued by very expensive trouble. While refitting in Hoboken, New Jersey, in the early morning of October 15, 1918, she promptly listed to port. Sleeping soldiers and sailors onboard fled the ship in any way they could, but four soldiers and two sailors died. Righted by counter flooding, raised, and then refloated shortly after the armistice, she was repaired and resumed her duties of bringing troops home from Europe. (Courtesy of the Naval History and Heritage Command, Photo Archives, from the Naval Historical Foundation, Washington, DC.)

In 1921, the Navy transferred the SS *America* to the United States Line to resume her original function as a passenger liner. But only a few days before she was to be returned to the company after undergoing repairs and renovations at Newport News Shipyard and Dry Dock Company, she caught fire on March 26, 1926. She burned for seven hours, primarily in the passenger cabin sections, causing some $2 million in damage. The *America* was rebuilt and resumed her Atlantic passenger routes with the United States Line until 1931, when was anchored in the James River as a reserve transport. With war again erupting in Europe, she was returned to her final service in October 1940 as the troopship USAT *Edmund B. Alexander.* Though she served faithfully, she soon became redundant and was scrapped in 1957. (Courtesy of The Mariners' Museum and Park.)

Vessels destroyed by fire or made redundant are often salvaged for their iron and other commodities, as was the case with the *Accomac*. She was built as the *Virginia Lee* in 1928 for ferry service across the lower Eastern Shore to Norfolk for the Pennsylvania Railroad. After service with the Navy during World War II, she was converted to diesel, and as *Holiday*, she served as a ferry between Boston and Provincetown. Returned to the southern Chesapeake Bay, she was converted to an end-loading ferry and renamed *Accomac*. She carried passengers and vehicles across the mouth of the Chesapeake Bay as part of the Virginia Ferry Corporation and thus was a vital link for residents of the lower Eastern Shore of Virginia. But she lost her raison d'être when the Chesapeake Bay Bridge Tunnel opened in 1964. (Courtesy of the Steamship Historical Society of America.)

The *Accomac*'s owners hoped that she would continue as a ferry. But while being refitted at Pinners Point in Portsmouth, Virginia, on the night of May 27, 1964, fire broke out, spread quickly, and destroyed the *Accomac*. She was eventually towed to Mallows Bay on the Potomac River (see pages 111–115), where she remains in full view. (Author's collection.)

Deadly fires and explosions are not reserved exclusively to commercial or war vessels. They can and do occur on pleasure boats of all sizes, often with disastrous results. On Saturday evening, October 4, 1941, Dr. James Pancoast, a well-known and successful physician in Germantown, Pennsylvania, was taking advantage of the end of the summer boating season with family and friends on his yacht *Kooyang* at the end of a 75-foot dock on the Sassafras River in Fredericktown, Maryland. It is believed that a hidden leak caused propane gas to collect in the boat's bilge, and as the party was readying her, the gas was ignited by a spark. The boat was violently blown apart, with most of those onboard thrown into the water with devastating injuries. In all, three were killed and seven injured. (Courtesy of the Chesapeake Bay Maritime Museum, gift of Tucker Moorshead.)

Fires do not always occur at sea; many happen when the vessel is tied up in harbor. The *Old Point Comfort*, built in 1886 in Wilmington, Delaware, initially saw service across the mouth of the Chesapeake Bay carrying train cars between the terminus for the rail line down the Delmarva Peninsula at Cape Charles, Virginia, and Norfolk. From 1904 to 1907, she was owned by the James River Day Line and steamed between Norfolk and Richmond, Virginia. In 1907, she was bought by the Baltimore, Chesapeake & Atlantic Railroad. (Courtesy of The Mariners' Museum and Park.)

On August 22, 1920, while at Pier 1 on Pratt Street in Baltimore, the 34-year-old steamer caught fire, burned to the waterline, and sank. (Courtesy of the Steamship Historical Society of America.)

She was raised, sold, and stripped of her ferryboat configuration, then converted to a barge until she was eventually abandoned in 1936. (Courtesy of The Mariners' Museum and Park.)

One very tragic shipboard explosion on the Potomac River killed a secretary of state and a secretary of the Navy and nearly killed the president of the United States. The USS *Princeton*, launched in 1843, was the Navy's newest and most technologically advanced ship, using a screw propeller. She also carried two huge 12-inch guns able to fire 225-pound shells up to five miles with a 50-pound powder charge. They were named the "Oregon" and the "Peacemaker." The latter was then the largest naval gun in the world, weighing 27,000 pounds and forever holding a special place in explosion history. (Courtesy of the Naval History and Heritage Command, Photo Archives.)

Capt. Robert Stockton, one of the leading proponents for improvements in naval technology, was behind building the USS *Princeton*. The ship was named for his home in New Jersey, and he was her first captain. Stockton contracted with an inventive but cantankerous genius, Swedish immigrant John Ericsson, to design the two large and powerful guns. Sadly, Stockton rushed the guns' development, interfering with Ericsson's better technical understanding of the engineering. (Courtesy of the US Senate Historical Office.)

John Ericsson was one of the great inventors of the 19th century. While difficult and opinionated—resulting in a long-standing legal fight with Stockton and the Navy over what happened on the USS *Princeton*—he would make a revolutionary contribution to naval warfare in 1862 with the design and construction of the USS *Monitor* (see page 90). (Courtesy of the Naval History and Heritage Command, Photo Archives.)

AWFUL EXPLOSION of the *"PEACE-MAKER"* on board the U.S. STEAM FRIGATE. *PRINCETON*, on WEDNESDAY, 28TH FEB! 1844.

To show off his new ship and cannons, Stockton took officials down the Potomac River on the *Princeton* to witness a demonstration of the Peacemaker. On February 28, 1844, with Pres. John Tyler and some 400 leading dignitaries on board, including former first lady Dolly Madison, Stockton fired the Peacemaker several times without incident. Then Navy Secretary Thomas Gilmer requested another firing. Fortunately, President Tyler was below when the Peacemaker exploded, owing to stress on the poorly made breech, throwing red-hot pieces of iron through the observers. When the dense smoke cleared, the bodies of the dead and injured littered the deck. Six died, and about 20 were injured, including Stockton. A Navy board of inquiry absolved Stockton of any wrongdoing, likely owing to his family's connections and influence. The disaster, though deadly, did lead to new techniques for stronger and more structurally sound cannons. (Courtesy of the Naval History and Heritage Command, Photo Archives.)

The oil tanker *Mantilla* was originally from Tønsberg, Norway, displaced about 8,400 tons, and was operated by the Mexican Petroleum Company primarily on the Tampico-Baltimore run. In 1926, she put into the dry dock at Sparrows Point, Baltimore, to undergo repairs and some reconditioning. Work included the use of acetylene torches amidships that unfortunately came in contact with what was believed to have been a gas buildup in the fuel tank. (Courtesy of the Steamship Historical Society of America.)

Shortly before noon on Friday, November 19, 1926, a huge explosion catapulted steel and burning oil over the aft section of the ship and into the surrounding neighborhoods. It blew out windows in nearby buildings, set fire to the ship, and sent an 8-foot-wide, 30-ton piece of steel onto the deck of the steamer *Mount Clary* in an adjoining dry dock. (Courtesy of *Fire Engineering*.)

The injured were rushed to local hospitals, many dying from their horrific wounds. The final death toll was 16, including the captain, Nils Danielson. (Courtesy of *Fire Engineering*.)

The second of three steamers named *Tolchester* operating in the Chesapeake was bought in 1933 by the Tolchester Steamboat Company. She served some eight years on the very fashionable 2-hour, 27-mile excursion run between Baltimore and the popular Tolchester Beach in Kent County, Maryland. The *Tolchester* was one of the most popular Bay excursion steamers, able to carry up to 2,200 passengers on special holiday parties. (Courtesy of The Mariners' Museum and Park.)

Beginning in the 1880s, as more and more of the public wanted leisure excursions, Tolchester Beach and Park grew to include hotels, restaurants, an amusement park, a merry-go-round, and a roller coaster, not to mention the ever-popular bathing and crabbing. The beach closed in 1962 owing to the increasing use of personal vehicles, segregation laws, and changing demographics. While this image shows the *Express* at Tolchester Beach, the steamer *Tolchester* also docked here. (Courtesy of The Mariners' Museum and Park.)

After several months undergoing repairs for the upcoming excursion season, the *Tolchester* was brought to the company's Light Street pier on Wednesday, May 14, 1941. At about 12:30 a.m. the following morning, fire broke out on the steamer and spread quickly to the pier. It ultimately became an eight-alarm fire with some 150 firemen and two fireboats fighting the inferno. Ten firemen were injured, but fortunately, there were no deaths. The popular *Tolchester* was damaged beyond repair, and she was subsequently sold and converted into a barge to carry pulpwood in Virginia. Her end came in 1964 when she was used as a bulkhead on the Elizabeth River in Berkley, Virginia. (With permission from the *Baltimore Sun*.)

With a similar history to the SS *America* (pages 15–17), the German passenger liner *George Washington* was launched on November 10, 1908, and was operated by the North Germany Lloyd Line until 1914. With the outbreak of World War I, she sought refuge in neutral New York City. When the United States entered the war in 1917, the liner was confiscated and converted to a troop transport. Over 18 round trips, she carried 48,000 troops to Europe and 34,000 back. Here, the *George Washington* steams up New York Harbor on July 8, 1919, with Pres. Woodrow Wilson on board returning from the Versailles peace negotiations. After resuming passenger service between the wars, she was used in World War II, transporting over 25,000 troops in both the Atlantic and Pacific until taken out of service in 1947. (Courtesy of the Naval History and Heritage Command, Photo Archives.)

The magnificent and once-proud *George Washington* met a sad and ignominious end. Tied up at Baltimore's Hawkins Point Ammunition Pier and loaded with machinery and supplies for use in the construction of the Chesapeake Bay Bridge, she was destroyed on January 16, 1951, by a huge 10-alarm fire. (With permission from the *Baltimore Sun*.)

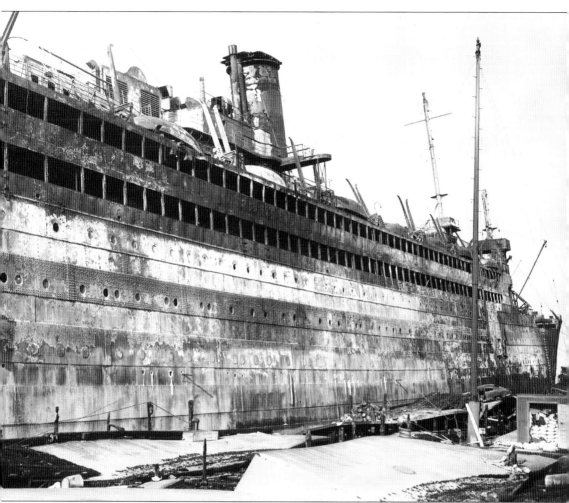

The fire that destroyed the *George Washington* became Baltimore's second most destructive fire. Besides the 25,000-ton ship, the fire also destroyed the Hawkins Point Ammunition Pier and damaged two barges, a tug, and a pile driver, with total losses estimated at over $15 million. The effort to fight the fire was made more difficult by high winds and freezing temperatures. Ironically, the old SS *America*, renamed the *Edmund B. Alexander*, was moored at the pier with the *George Washington* but was cut adrift in time to be saved. (With permission from the *Baltimore Sun*.)

Sadly, the *George Washington* was burned beyond any hope of repairs. She was towed to Curtis Bay, south of Baltimore, and sold for scrap a few weeks after the fire. (Courtesy of The Mariners' Museum and Park.)

The *Three Rivers*—named for the Patuxent, Potomac, and Rappahannock—was a steel-hulled, side-wheel passenger steamer built in 1910 at Sparrows Point, Baltimore. The first steamer with three decks, she was used on the Potomac River, then switched to the Baltimore–Crisfield, Maryland, run. But she suffered one of the most shocking and saddest catastrophes ever to take place on the Bay. (Courtesy of Jack Shaum.)

On the evening of July 4, 1924, she was returning to Baltimore from the annual workboat races at Crisfield. On board were 139, including 59 members of the *Baltimore Evening Sun's* newsboy band, who were between 12 and 17 years old. Shortly after midnight off Cove Point in Calvert County, fire broke out in the saloon and spread quickly. Panic ensued, and passengers leapt overboard, many without life preservers. Many of the boys alerted passengers in their cabins, threw life preservers to those in the water, and helped fight the fire. The bandleader wrote, "Many of the boys were among the last to leave the burning boat." The fire—hot enough to melt glass—destroyed the superstructure. Ten died, and 12 were injured. Tragically, half of the deaths were boys from the band. (Photograph by R.F. Kneisch; courtesy of the Chesapeake Bay Maritime Museum, gift of Peter Chambliss.)

The deceased newsboys were buried side by side in Loudon Park Cemetery in Baltimore, and the *Baltimore Evening Sun* erected a stone memorial with headstones for each of the five boys, Vernon Jefferson (15), Nelson Miles (12), Walter Millikin (13), Thomas Pilker Jr. (13), and Lester Seligman (15). (Author's collection.)

The *Three Rivers's* burned-out hull was raised and the machinery taken out. The owners wanted to sell her to the Tolchester Steamboat Company to be used as a ferry. The idea was discarded as unfeasible and likely unpopular in the Baltimore region. Instead, the empty hull was converted to a lumber-carrying barge and renamed the *Richmond Cedar Work No. 6*. She operated as such until stripped and abandoned in 1958. (Courtesy of The Mariners' Museum and Park.)

The *City of Baltimore*, built in 1911 for the Chesapeake Steamship Company, was a very popular passenger ferry up and down the Bay. Both she and her sister ship the *City of Norfolk* were full three-deckers, 300 feet long, steel-hulled, and intended to compete more successfully against the line's primary rival, the Old Bay Line. Both plied the lucrative Baltimore-Norfolk run, the *City of Baltimore* for 26 years. This image shows her leaving Norfolk. On the afternoon of Thursday, July 29, 1937, the *City of Baltimore* left Pier 5 and headed out of Baltimore on what would be her final voyage. (Courtesy of The Mariners' Museum and Park.)

She had about 150 passengers and crewmen aboard and was an hour out near Bodkin Point when passengers heard cries of fire from the crew. A powerful blast from the engine room went through the midsection, and flames quickly turned the *City of Baltimore* into an inferno. Witnesses said that the fire on the ship so lit up the Bay that it could be seen as far as seven miles away on shore. Only a single lifeboat was able to be launched. (Courtesy of The Mariners' Museum and Park.)

Accounts spoke of passengers hanging from the ship's sides to escape the flames, most dropping into the water as the fire and heat approached. Credit for saving many panic-stricken passengers was given to Capt. Charles Brooks, who forced them to don life belts. As the *City of Baltimore* burned ferociously, other steamers on the Bay began to arrive, as did a slew of small boats from shore. None, however, could get within 100 feet of the burning inferno but instead circled the steamer, picking up floating survivors in the firelight. Pres. Franklin Roosevelt, advised of the disaster in Washington, ordered ships sent from the Naval Academy in nearby Annapolis to assist, and the Coast Guard sent cutters from nearby stations. The Red Cross directed its chapters at Baltimore and Annapolis to send doctors and nurses. Given the devastation, it is nothing short of miraculous that only two people died, although many received injuries. The burned-out hulk was eventually towed to Baltimore and broken up. (Courtesy of The Mariners' Museum and Park.)

The steamship *Nantucket* was built in 1899 as a freight- and passenger-carrying vessel for the Merchants and Miners Transportation Company. She served many East Coast ports but was a regular on the Baltimore-Boston run. Arriving in Baltimore from one run, she discharged her passengers and some cargo and then proceeded to Pier 6 at Locust Point to discharge the rest of her cargo onto cars of the Baltimore & Ohio Railroad. On September 2, 1912, stevedores discovered a fire in her hold. Using shipboard equipment to try and extinguish the flames, their efforts proved futile, and it rapidly became a two-alarm fire for city firemen, assisted by tugs pumping water. (Courtesy of The Mariners' Museum and Park.)

Increasingly full of the water being poured onto her, the *Nantucket* became so top heavy that she suddenly capsized on her starboard side, forcing firemen and crew members to shimmy up the angled deck, holding onto any object they could find until rescued or able to make their own way to the pier. Two firemen perished, and several others were overcome by smoke. The *Nantucket* would suffer more drama less than two years later when she collided on January 13, 1914, with the Old Dominion Line's SS *Monroe* off Hog Island, Virginia, just north and outside the mouth of the Chesapeake Bay. Out of a total of 141 passengers and crew on the *Monroe*, 42 were tragically killed. When the *Nantucket* suffered another fire at Locust Point in Baltimore, she was no longer of value and was scrapped in November 1933. (Courtesy of The Mariners' Museum and Park.)

For shipbuilding companies, there is not much worse than a ship nearing completion being nearly destroyed by fire. The SS *Segovia*, a refrigerated freighter with accommodations for 100 passengers, was built by Newport News Shipbuilding and Dry Dock Company. Fire broke out in one of her holds at 4:30 a.m. on December 20, 1931, five weeks before her delivery date to her new owners. A strong breeze carried the fire into the passenger quarters, destroying the interior and making the ship difficult for firefighters to access. So much water poured into the No. 3 hold that by 7:00 a.m., the ship listed severely to starboard. One fireman was seriously burned; several more suffered minor injuries. The disaster could have been considerably worse had the fire spread to the *Segovia*'s sister ships the SS *Talamanca* and the SS *Chiriqui* being built at the next pier. (Courtesy of The Mariners' Museum and Park.)

The *Segovia* was repaired and renamed SS *Peten*. She was christened on August 15, 1932, by First Lady Lou Henry Hoover. During World War II, she was delivered to the US War Shipping Administration and converted for the Navy as the USS *Ariel*, seeing service in the Atlantic, Mediterranean, and Gulf of Mexico. In 1946, she returned to the United Fruit Company as the SS *Jamaica*. (Courtesy of The Mariners' Museum and Park.)

The steamer *Virginia* was built in Wilmington, Delaware, for the Baltimore Steam Packet Company (the Old Bay Line). In 1909, she was renovated, and her staterooms were extended astern on the gallery deck. Sadly, 10 years later, on May 24, 1919, the *Virginia* caught fire shortly after midnight off Smith's Point, Virginia, with 156 passengers and a crew of 82 onboard heading to Newport News to welcome soldiers returning from overseas following World War I. (Courtesy of The Mariners' Museum and Park.)

With these steamers and their wooden superstructures, flames spread with extraordinary speed, stoked by the breezes coming off the water. The passengers panicked in the dark as they struggled and groped to find a lifeboat, some of which capsized while loading passengers. Fortunately, the waters were calm that night, which allowed for successful rescue efforts when several other steamers arrived, including the *City of Norfolk* and the *City of Annapolis*. The *Virginia's* captain, Walter G. Lane, remained with his ship to the end but suffered burns. Five passengers and one crewman were lost. Seen in this photograph, the *Virginia's* hulk was towed by commercial fishermen to the mouth of the Great Wicomico River; they tried unsuccessfully to claim salvage of the wreck. She was eventually scrapped in Baltimore. (Courtesy of Jack Shaum.)

Local passenger and freight service between Washington, DC, and a multitude of small landings on the Potomac River was not only commonplace but necessary and profitable. One vessel on this run was the *Wawaset*, a steam sidewheeler of about 350 tons owned by the Potomac Ferry Company, which ran a weekly service. Drawing about four feet, the *Wawaset* could get close to those smaller landings that had no dock or wharf and used rowboats to ferry passengers and cargoes. With her machinery recently overhauled, the *Wawaset* left Washington, DC, at 6:00 a.m. on August 8, 1873, with about 145 passengers—about half women and children—and a crew of 12. Just as she was reaching Chatterton's Landing in King William's County, Virginia, a fire smoldering in the steamer's hold ignited, and it engulfed the vessel when hatches were opened and air fed the fire. Passengers panicked, and the *Wawaset* ran aground a couple hundred yards offshore. (Courtesy of the National Archives.)

Passengers rushed for lifeboats being lowered, but in the panic, the boats overturned, and passengers began jumping overboard. Despite the availability of life preservers, few secured them as the steamer burned to the waterline. Waiting relatives and friends on shore did what they could to save lives. No accurate record of the dead has been determined, but recent scholarship suggests that over 70 died. This kind of tragedy quickly resulted in images like this one from the August 12, 1873, edition of the *Daily Graphic* of New York. (Courtesy of the National Archives.)

Following the tragedy, some of the victims of the *Wawaset* disaster were buried in the Congressional Cemetery in Washington, DC. (Courtesy of the Library of Congress.)

Another favorite steamboat during the heyday of Bay steamers was the *Love Point*. Built as the *Emma A. Ford* in 1884 for the Chester River Steamboat Company, she ran freight and passenger excursions to and from the Chester River on Maryland's Eastern Shore. The company's president, Budd Sterling Ford, named the boat after his wife. The *Emma A. Ford's* interior was described on May 10, 1884, by the *Kent News* as "tastefully decorated . . . the upholstery . . . crimson silk plush. The wood work in the lady's saloon is in cherry." Bought by the Maryland, Delaware & Virginia Railway Company, the *Emma A. Ford* was rechristened *Love Point* in 1906 for the northern tip of Kent Island, Maryland, and the entrance to the Chester River, where the steamer frequently stopped. (Courtesy of Henry F. Rimm.)

The *Love Point* was rebuilt with more deck space for passengers after a fire in 1906. Fire broke out again at the dock at Love Point on the night of March 11, 1909. Fortunately, only the crew was aboard, and all managed to escape unharmed. But sadly, the boat was completely destroyed. The hulk was salvaged and used as a barge, then abandoned in 1952 off Leading Point in Curtis Bay south of Baltimore. She was later moved nearer shore and filled with dirt to serve as a bulkhead. (Courtesy of Ann Ervin.)

Another favorite Chester River Steamboat Company steamer was the *B.S. Ford*, shown in August 1893. Launched in 1877 as one of the most advanced passenger vessels plying the Bay, she had a smoking room and a lady's parlor and could accommodate 400 passengers. Her triangular dining room could serve 200 at one seating. Named for Budd Sterling Ford, who was also a Maryland delegate and later state senator from Queen Anne's County, she became one of the longest lasting steamboats in Chesapeake Bay history with runs primarily between Baltimore and Chestertown, Maryland. (Courtesy of The Mariners' Museum and Park.)

Immediately after a major overhaul that included new paint and interior furnishings, fire broke out early on May 5, 1884, at Chestertown. Three crewmen escaped harm, but her superstructure was destroyed. Rebuilt and modified in Baltimore to carry additional freight, the *B.S. Ford* was sold in 1929 and converted to diesel power for use throughout the Bay. She was rammed and sunk off Old Point Comfort, Virginia, on June 7, 1936, by the *District of Columbia* (see pages 64–67). The *B.S. Ford* was raised and became one of the mid-Atlantic's largest timber barges, able to carry 250,000 board-feet. On October 23, 1960, she ran aground at the mouth of the Honga River in Dorchester County, Maryland, and sank, ending her 83-year career. (Courtesy of the Chesapeake Bay Maritime Museum, Robert H. Burgess Collection.)

Two

COLLISIONS

Next to explosions and fires, collision with other ships and vessels, as well as with stationary objects like markers, buoys, and shoals was—and is—another major reason for shipwrecks. One can well image how many unrecorded shipwrecks occurred in the Chesapeake Bay since the early 17th century owing to collisions with other vessels or—perhaps more likely—grounding on shoals and projections of land, especially before the days of radio communication or such aids as channel markers.

Clearly, and not unlike improvements in fire prevention and firefighting methods in more recent times, better navigational aids like markers, buoys, and more accurate charts, as well as new technologies like radar and global positioning satellites, have decreased the number of collisions. This is true for the larger commercial and passenger vessels as well as for smaller recreational ones. But while improvements in technologies and navigational aids have helped, these very same improvements have resulted in sea lanes becoming more congested and ships traveling at higher speeds. These factors increase the probability of a collision between two vessels or with shore or offshore structures. And as modern ships are larger and carry far more commodities, collisions can result in huge impacts on the environment. In earlier days, ships carried far less cargo, and when it spilled into the water, it had less effect on the Bay's environment.

But whatever technological improvements are made, and no matter the amount of proper training and safety steps taken to avoid collisions, they can only be as effective as the people using them. Human error remains ever-present, and the Chesapeake Bay continues to see collisions—sadly, some with deadly consequences.

The *City of Annapolis* and the *City of Richmond* (below) were sister ships built in 1913 in Baltimore. The excursion steamers operated on reciprocal courses between Baltimore and West Point, Virginia, on the York River, normally passing each other near the mouth of the Potomac River. (Courtesy of The Mariners' Museum and Park.)

The *City of Richmond*, while having a stellar reputation for passenger comfort and style, nevertheless suffered several collisions and mishaps in her career. (Courtesy of The Mariners' Museum and Park.)

Both the *City of Annapolis* and the *City of Richmond* were modernized in the 1920s and subsequently described as palatial, containing the latest safety equipment, electric lights, and private staterooms. (Courtesy of The Mariners' Museum and Park.)

On June 19, 1915, at the West Point pier, the *City of Richmond* rather ignominiously and embarrassingly sank. She was raised and repaired, only to sink again four months later when she collided with the Chesapeake Bay schooner *James H. Hargrove* off Point No Point, Maryland. She would again suffer minor damage in another collision in Baltimore Harbor. (Courtesy of The Mariners' Museum and Park.)

Sadly, the *City of Richmond* is best known for colliding with and sinking the *City of Annapolis*. During the night of February 23–24, 1927, while heading south, she suddenly hit fog, reducing visibility to several hundred feet. As the two steamers approached each other, they signaled their presence, but as later described, the fog altered the signals. The *City of Richmond* plowed into the *City of Annapolis's* port-side staterooms, instantly killing 20-year-old passenger Virginia Starkey. The *City of Annapolis* was abandoned, the remaining 100 passengers and crew climbing aboard the *City of Richmond* before pulling free of her sinking sister ship. With a caved-in bow but watertight, the *City of Richmond* returned to Baltimore with her double load. Amidst accusations of fault, both captains were fined $50 and saw their licenses revoked for a year. The accident-prone *City of Richmond* was eventually sold to become a hotel-restaurant in the Virgin Islands but was lost while under tow and sank on October 5, 1964, in heavy seas off Georgetown, South Carolina. (Courtesy of The Mariners' Museum and Park.)

Those who earn their living fishing know how dangerous collisions can be, since fishing boats operate in all kinds of weather and conditions. The menhaden trawler *Benjamin O. Colonna*, based out of Reedville, Virginia, was returning in the predawn hours of October 26, 1948, with 21 crewmen when she encountered heavy fog. Meanwhile, the 10,296-ton tanker SS *Tullahoma*—bound to Baltimore full of crude oil—suddenly found the *Colonna* veering directly across the tanker's path between the Patuxent and Potomac Rivers. At 4:42 a.m., the *Tullahoma* rammed the trawler and cut her in half. (Courtesy of the Reedville Fishermen's Museum.)

The *Colonna's* aft section sank almost immediately; the forward section capsized but remained afloat. The *Tullahoma* promptly notified the Coast Guard, which launched lifeboats, picking up 16 survivors. Two cutters and an airplane searched for the other five crewmen, but despite their efforts, the others were never found. This is the last image of the forward section of the *Benjamin O. Colonna* before it sank. (Courtesy of the Reedville Fishermen's Museum.)

The *Emma Giles*, one of the most familiar and popular sidewheelers based out of Baltimore, was operated by the Tolchester Steamboat Company from Baltimore to docks and piers all over the mid-Chesapeake, including Annapolis, Tolchester Beach, West River, Rhode River, Shady Side, and Port Deposit. Off Sandy Point at about 8:00 p.m. on January 1, 1924, she was returning to Baltimore and plowing through heavy fog when she collided with a freighter. (Photograph by R.L. Graham; courtesy of the Chesapeake Bay Maritime Museum, gift of H.G. Wood.)

The SS *Steel Trader*, an 8,000-ton freighter owned by US Steel, was too much for the aging steamer. Both captains signaled their presence and confirmed each other's intention of a starboard-to-starboard passing. However, once the two neared each other, despite their efforts to avoid meeting, the ships collided. (Courtesy of Skip Lewis.)

The *Steel Trader* raked the starboard side of the *Emma Giles*, destroying 250 square feet of her deckhouse planking, shredding the starboard paddle box to the hub, and jamming the paddle blades so that the wheel could not turn, essentially making her dead in the water. Fortunately, none of the 52 passengers and crew on the *Emma Giles* was injured. The freighter then slowly towed the *Emma Giles* to Baltimore. Subsequent investigations blamed the weather for the collision, and the captain and crew of the *Steel Trader* were commended for their prompt and effective assistance to the stricken steamboat. (With permission from the *Baltimore Sun*.)

The *Emma Giles* is pictured while docked in Baltimore before her conversion to a barge. (Courtesy of The Mariners' Museum and Park.)

By 1936, the excursion trade began to wane on the Chesapeake Bay, and companies had increasing difficulties making profits. As such, it was decided that the *Emma Giles* would be converted to a barge. This image of her tied up in Baltimore shows the conversion to her new purpose. (With permission from the *Baltimore Sun*.)

By 1952, the *Emma Giles* ceased her useful life and was towed to the Baltimore area's graveyard for abandoned boats and vessels, Curtis Bay, where she was added to the already numerous derelict vessels there. She was burned in order to salvage the iron. As late as 2005, her stern was still visible and ironically bore the painted sign "Free to good home." (Photograph by Robert H. Burgess; courtesy of the Chesapeake Bay Maritime Museum, Robert H. Burgess Collection.)

Collisions also occur between relatively small vessels, sometimes with tragic loss of life. The USS *Minnesota* was present in Hampton Roads for the Jamestown Exposition to celebrate the 300th anniversary of the Jamestown colony from April to December 1907. Many of the social activities were at Sewell's Point in Norfolk, an exciting tour of duty for young officers and seamen especially. (Courtesy of the Naval History and Heritage Command, Photo Archives.)

The crew used steam launches like this one to go to and from shore. On the night of June 10, 1907, a storm came up rapidly while a launch was returning from an Army-Navy ball in Norfolk carrying six Naval Academy midshipmen and six crewmen back to the *Minnesota*. When the launch failed to show up, searchers combed the waters until, sadly, bodies and pieces of the launch were found a few days later. The launch had tried to pass a tug, but the coxswain failed to see the barge being towed by the tug and rammed into the steel towing cable, killing all 12 on board. (Courtesy of the Naval History and Heritage Command, Photo Archives.)

The midshipmen who died were, from left to right (above) Philip H. Field, class of 1906, from Denver, Colorado; Franklin Portens Holcomb, class of 1907, from Newcastle, Delaware; and Herbert Leander Holden, class of 1907, from Portage, Wisconsin; (below) Clay Murfin Jr., class of 1907, from Jackson, Ohio; William Hollister Stevenson, class of 1906, from New Bern, North Carolina; and Walter Carl Ulrich, class of 1907, from Milwaukee, Wisconsin. (Both, courtesy of the US Naval Academy Museum.)

Vessels of all shapes and sizes ply the Chesapeake Bay. In a collision between a sailing schooner and a large steel freighter, which will receive the worst of it is a foregone conclusion. The *Herbert D. Maxwell* was a beautiful, 186-foot, four-masted schooner. Loaded in Baltimore with 1,150 tons of fertilizer for Wilmington, North Carolina, and with a crew of nine, the schooner anchored off the Magothy River due to light winds. By 3:00 a.m. on March 16, 1912, and with a fresh breeze, the schooner sailed across the Bay toward Kent Island. (Courtesy of Cowcard.)

At about 4:45 a.m., she was rammed by the SS *Gloucester*, a 2,541-ton steamer heading for Baltimore. The *Herbert D. Maxwell* sank in about 70 feet of water off Kent Island near today's Bay Bridge. Four crew members were killed, while the surviving five were rescued by the *Gloucester* after floating on wreckage. Accusations of blame came from both sides, and the court eventually declared both equally responsible. With little to salvage, the beautiful *Herbert D. Maxwell* was deemed to be no hazard to navigation and subsequently left where she rested. (Courtesy of the Steamship Historical Society of America.)

Collisions between two freighters can also be deadly. Built in 1882, the *Julia Luckenbach* was a three-decker freighter with passengers steaming up the Chesapeake Bay toward Baltimore. At the same time, the newer and much larger steamer *Indrakuala* left Baltimore headed south. With heavy fog on the morning of January 3, 1913, though both ships sounded their horns, they nevertheless collided off the Tangier Light. The *Luckenbach* sank in less than two minutes, while the *Indrakuala* grounded herself to prevent sinking. (Courtesy of the Steamship Historical Society of America.)

Passengers and crew members on the *Luckenbach* scrambled to save themselves, which was made more complicated by the arrival of a ferocious gale. Several crewmen climbed the ship's rigging, still above the now-churning waterline. Eight crewmen on the masts were eventually rescued by a passing ship after being stranded for 15 hours. These eight and six more were saved, but 15 people died. This image is from the January 7, 1913, *New Brunswick Times*. (Courtesy of Michael W. Pocock, www.maritimequest.com.)

63

The *District of Columbia* was a steel screw-propeller passenger ship built in 1925. On the morning of October 31, 1948, having called at Old Point Comfort, Virginia, from Washington, DC, she headed across Hampton Roads on the last lap to Norfolk. But in doing so, she encountered fog. Nearby was the tanker *Georgia*. Both ships used their bells, but the fog and a strong flood tide distorted the sound, and the two ships collided. The *District of Columbia* was run aground on Hampton Bar to avoid sinking. While most passengers were awake and having breakfast, sadly one woman in her berth was killed and three others injured. (Courtesy of the Steamship Historical Society of America.)

The tanker's steel bow raked a huge gash along the *District of Columbia's* starboard wooden superstructure. The collision spelled the doom of her owners, the old Norfolk and Washington Steamboat Company, already in financial difficulties. She was taken over in the following year by the Old Bay Line, which repaired her, and she continued to operate out of Washington, DC, until 1957, when she was moved to Baltimore and became a backup steamer on the night run between Baltimore and Norfolk. (Courtesy of The Mariners' Museum and Park.)

With the demise of the Old Bay Line in 1962, the steamer, now renamed *Provincetown*, was a cruise ferry between Boston and Provincetown during the summers of 1962 and 1963. She was purchased and returned to Baltimore with plans to resume operations on the Chesapeake Bay, but costly US Coast Guard safety requirements put an end to those plans. She lay idle at Baltimore's Pratt Street Pier 3, during which a deal was negotiated to convert her into a New Jersey shoreside restaurant. Those plans literally went up in smoke when vandals set fire to her on June 4, 1969. She quickly became a six-alarm blaze with over 230 firemen and two Baltimore fireboats struggling to put out the flames. (With permission from the *Baltimore Sun*.)

The burned-out hulk was towed to the dead anchorage in Curtis Bay, where the old *District of Columbia* continued to deteriorate until she sank and disappeared in 1971. (Courtesy of Jack Shaum.)

A steel-hulled passenger ship launched in September 1922 by the Old Bay Line, the *State of Virginia* provided overnight steamboat service primarily between Baltimore and Norfolk, making one of the fastest nonstop runs between those cities: 10 hours and 3 minutes. (Courtesy of The Mariners' Museum and Park.)

Returning to Baltimore on July 14, 1936, following a two-day excursion by 235 reveling conventioneers of the Maryland Automobile Trade Association, the *State of Virginia* was nearing the Patapsco River when, about 8:30 p.m., passengers were thrown to the decks by a huge crash. The bow of the large freighter *Golden Harvest* slammed some 10 feet into the port side of the *State of Virginia*. Remarkably, no one was seriously injured, and passengers were landed in Baltimore on the following morning. The two ships were so tightly connected that it took shipyard workers with acetylene torches to separate them. Both were ultimately repaired and returned to service. (Courtesy of The Mariners' Museum and Park.)

At the time of the collision, most conventioneers, including Maryland's rotund governor, Henry W. Nice (front right with sunglasses), were in the forward saloon watching a rather raucous and rowdy chorus-girl show. When the ships collided, panic swept the room, with girls screaming and some passengers kneeling and praying. Calm was restored when the crew assured the passengers that the ship was safe and would not sink. (With permission from the *Baltimore Sun*.)

By October 1978, the cutter *Cuyahoga* was the oldest commissioned vessel in US Coast Guard service. Built in 1927 to intercept rumrunners during Prohibition, she served as the tender to Pres. Franklin D. Roosevelt's yacht, the USS *Potomac*. The *Cuyahoga* saw duty during World War II on the East Coast, much of it dealing with the training of young officer candidates. Following the war, she returned to patrol work. Her normal complement was a crew of 29 men. (Courtesy of the US Coast Guard Heritage Assets Collection and Archives.)

The *Cuyahoga* came to a tragic end on October 20, 1978. On a night-time training cruise heading north in the Chesapeake off the Potomac River and cruising at 12 knots in clear weather, the crew sighted a light to the north and assumed the contact was a small northbound vessel. Instead, the light proved to be the 521-foot bulk freighter *Santa Cruz II*, carrying over 19,000 tons of coal and traveling south at over 14 knots. This image shows the freighter's bow with the rather minimal damage she suffered in the collision with the *Cuyahoga*. (With permission from the *Baltimore Sun*.)

The two ships were correctly passing port-to-port. When they were 1,200 yards apart, the *Cuyahoga* suddenly turned west into the Potomac River to moor for the night. This turn took them directly into the freighter's path. At 9:07 p.m., the bulbous underwater bow of the *Santa Cruz II* tore through the *Cuyahoga* amidships, rolling the cutter over at a 50-degree angle. She sank in two minutes in 58 feet of water. Rescue vessels arrived, but of the 29 Coast Guardsmen on board, 11 died, most being in the berthing areas or in the engine room, which took the collision's main impact. The *Cuyahoga* was raised and towed to Portsmouth. The Coast Guard decided to take the very old, badly damaged cutter 15 miles offshore, where she was scuttled as an artificial fishing reef. The casualty report on July 31, 1979, concluded that the *Cuyahoga* failed to identify the freighter's navigation lights and, not seeing that the vessels were on a collision course, failed to alter course. Every year there is a memorial to the victims at the Coast Guard station in Yorktown, Virginia. (Courtesy of the US Coast Guard Heritage Assets Collection and Archives.)

When large freighters and smaller—often passenger—vessels meet physically, it never goes well for the smaller ship. Such was the case with the SS *Powhatan*. Beginning in 1894 as the SS *Yorktown*, an iron-hulled passenger ship for the Old Dominion Steamship Company, she was primarily used for the Norfolk–New York City run. (Courtesy of the Naval History and Heritage Command, Photo Archives.)

Shortly after her launch, the Navy, needing ships to transport men and matériel for the Spanish-American War, commissioned her on April 21, 1898, as the USS *Resolute* to serve as an auxiliary cruiser and transport. As the Army transport *Rawlings* in early 1900, her troubles began. On April 10, 1901, she caught fire and sank in Brooklyn, New York, when about to sail to Havana. She was repaired, sold to the Merchants and Miners Transportation Company, renamed *Powhatan*, and used on the Norfolk–New England run. (Courtesy of the Naval History and Heritage Command, Photo Archives.)

This photograph of passengers near the pilothouse clearly enjoying their time on the *Powhatan* was taken in October 1915. The thought of a disaster happening a little over a year later was on no one's mind. (Courtesy of The Mariners' Museum and Park.)

On December 15, 1916, the outbound *Powhatan* collided with the larger inbound British tanker *Telena* southeast of Thimble Shoal Light on the lower Chesapeake Bay. The *Powhatan* was promptly beached but was initially believed to be a total loss. But with America's entry into World War I five months later, demands for shipping resulted in her hulk being raised. In 1919, she was converted into the first electric luxury passenger and freight ship. She ran between Florida and Cuba with the Miami Steamship Company. Renamed *Seneca*, she eventually burned and sank in December 1927 at Hoboken, New Jersey, and was scrapped. (Courtesy of The Mariners' Museum and Park.)

This image shows the bow damage to the tanker *Telena*, which was much larger than the *Powhatan*. She is being repaired in dry dock at Newport News Shipbuilding in Newport News, not far from where the collision occurred. (Courtesy of The Mariners' Museum and Park.)

Three

WAR

Today's popular perception of the Chesapeake Bay—held by those who use the Bay as a resource for food, a transit for goods and wares, or as a playground for recreational boating and sailing—rarely includes the fact that it has been a site of military conflicts. The famous "Oyster Wars" saw periodic and generally modest violence, but in fact, the Bay has not only been the venue of competing military forces, it has seen several rather large and historic military confrontations as well as many smaller fights and skirmishes.

In 1781, one of the most important military actions that ultimately resulted in the end of the American Revolution and the independence of the American colonies occurred in the Chesapeake Bay: the victory over the British at Yorktown. While the battle was primarily a siege of the British army by a combined Franco-American force, it is doubtful the allied forces would have been successful had a naval action a month before just outside the mouth of the Chesapeake not resulted in a French victory over the British.

A little over three decades later, in the War of 1812, several prominent actions took place in the Chesapeake Bay and its tributaries. Seeing its strategic and military value, Britain sent a force up the Bay to seize Washington, DC, then move on to take Baltimore. The American success at Baltimore and the story of Fort McHenry are well known to Americans. But the efforts at resisting the British moving up the Patuxent River toward the American capital are less well known. The gallant but unsuccessful effort by an overmatched American naval force led to one of the great underwater archaeological efforts to find and study Chesapeake Bay shipwrecks.

But it was during the Civil War—when the Chesapeake Bay was used by opposing forces—that the greatest number of military conflicts occurred on the Bay. Besides the hundreds of fights and skirmishes taking place up and down the Bay and its rivers, the Battle of Hampton Roads in March 1862 was not only important for the war's outcome but in fact resulted in a revolution in naval technology and warfare.

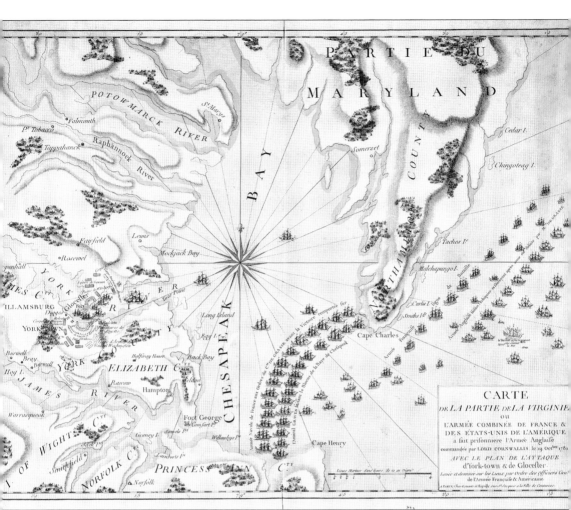

Unbeknownst to most participants, the American Revolution was about to see its final major battle in the late summer of 1781. The large but now exhausted British army under Gen. Charles Earl Cornwallis, having spent a long and difficult campaign in the southern colonies, moved north to Yorktown to await resupplying by the Royal Navy. The only hope for Cornwallis's army, now besieged by a growing Franco-American force and ably blockaded by a large French fleet, was the arrival of a British naval force. But when that force arrived, it was met and soundly defeated by the French navy on September 5, 1781, just outside the mouth of the Chesapeake Bay in the Battle of the Virginia Capes. (Courtesy of The Mariners' Museum and Park.)

THE APOLLO FRIGATE, OF 44 GUNS, GOING BEFORE THE WIND.
Published 1st July 1795, by LAURIE & WHITTLE, 53, Fleet Street, London.

Despite their increasingly desperate situation, the British still had about 60 smaller ships anchored off Yorktown that were scuttled to prevent the Franco-American forces from attacking from the water. As the allied forces applied greater pressure on the British from land and from water, the remaining British ships were bombarded with superheated cannonballs that ignited the wooden ships. One of Cornwallis's ships, the largest then off Yorktown, was the 44-gun HMS *Charon*. Sadly, no image of the *Charon* is known to exist, but this image of the HMS *Apollo* is an excellent example of the size, type, and configuration of the *Charon*. (Courtesy of the National Maritime Museum, Greenwich, London.)

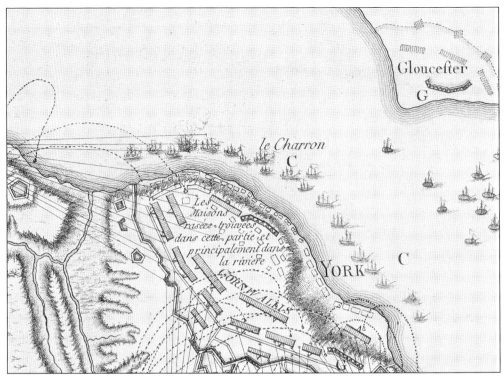

Coming under intense attack by American and French artillery, the *Charon* caught fire, drifted across the York River toward Gloucester, and, burning to the waterline, sank with considerable loss of life. With no possible relief from the British fleet, the destruction of the vessels off Yorktown, and the increasing pressure from the besiegers, Cornwallis was trapped and had no opportunity to extricate his army. He surrendered on October 19, 1781—a defeat that would spell the end of the war and the creation of an independent United States. (Courtesy of The Mariners' Museum and Park.)

There was much looting of the ships sunk off Yorktown and Gloucester Point following the battle. A serious and professional effort was made by underwater archeologists in the 1970s to discover Cornwallis's "Sunken Fleet." The vessels' remains were found in muddy waters and rather well preserved, including the hull of the *Charon*, from which artifacts were recovered, including this pewter tankard, now in the possession of The Mariners' Museum in Newport News. (Courtesy of The Mariners' Museum and Park.)

By 1814, Britain was determined to victoriously end the War of 1812. The Chesapeake Bay proved the ideal route to capture the republic's capital, Washington, DC, and eliminate places on the Chesapeake—including Baltimore—used by American privateers to raid British commerce. In a gallant but desperate effort, Commodore Joshua Barney, a naval hero from the American Revolution, hastily built a flotilla of shallow-draft barges to stall the British, then retreated to the safety of shoal waters abundant in the Chesapeake. (Courtesy of the Naval History and Heritage Command, Photo Archives.)

In June 1814, Barney's flotilla was met by a vastly superior British fleet and forced to retreat up the Patuxent River, where Barney burned and scuttled his barges and gunboats in St. Leonard's Creek to prevent their capture. He and his sailors then marched ahead of the British to Washington. They were among the few who put up a serious defense of the capital at the Battle of Bladensburg, where the Americans were routed. Modern efforts by archaeologists from the Navy and from Maryland's Patuxent River Park will hopefully uncover the remains of this gallant flotilla of American gunboats. (Courtesy of The Mariners' Museum and Park.)

America's worst naval disaster until Pearl Harbor was the burning and scuttling of many of the Navy's best ships in April 1861 at the Gosport Navy Yard across from Norfolk. Begun in 1767, the yard had the nation's first operational dry dock, and at the outset of the Civil War in 1861, it was the Navy's largest industrial facility. Secessionists immediately recognized the yard as a major target. For Unionists, its loss would spell disaster. (Courtesy of the Naval History and Heritage Command, Photo Archives.)

Upon Virginia's secession, Confederate forces were confident that the Navy yard could be easily taken. Union leadership at Gosport was uncoordinated and ineffective. On April 20, 1861, believing that he could defend neither the yard nor the warships in the harbor, the Navy's commander, Charles Stewart McCauley, ordered everything burned to prevent it falling into Confederate hands. Despite several significant Union ships, including the USS *Merrimack* and USS *Pennsylvania*, burning before Union forces evacuated, the effort was ultimately unsuccessful, and the Navy yard fell to the Confederacy. In all, 11 Union ships were sunk that night, but the Confederates were able to take nearly 1,200 heavy guns and large amounts of war matériel. (Courtesy of the Naval History and Heritage Command, Photo Archives.)

In addition to ships and war matériel, another huge loss for the Union was the dry dock at the Gosport Yard. This illustration was made to commemorate the opening in 1834. The dry dock would become critically important to one of the ships burned in April 1861 when the *Merrimack* was converted to an ironclad—an effort that would create a frightening new weapon for the Confederacy the following spring. (Courtesy of the Naval History and Heritage Command, Photo Archives.)

When the Navy yard was retaken by Union forces in May 1862, it was again burned and devastated—this time by fleeing Confederates. This photograph, taken immediately after the war, clearly shows the devastation of the Gosport Navy Yard. (Courtesy of the Naval History and Heritage Command, Photo Archives.)

One ship burned at Gosport in April 1861 would become famous after a radical transformation. The USS *Merrimack*, commissioned in 1856, was the first of six screw frigates in the US Navy. Seeing service in Europe and the Caribbean, she became the flagship of the Navy's Pacific Squadron before returning to Gosport Navy Yard and being placed in ordinary in early 1860. With the secession of Virginia, the *Merrimack* found herself blockaded, and was burned to her waterline and sunk in the Union's efforts to deny the yard and its ships to the Confederacy. (Courtesy of the Naval History and Heritage Command, Photo Archives.)

Without any significant warships of their own, the Confederates raised the *Merrimack* and, using the yard's dry dock, rebuilt the frigate into an entirely new weapon—the ironclad ram. Commissioned the CSS *Virginia* on February 17, 1862, she became the hope of the Confederacy to redress the balance of naval power in Hampton Roads, then dominated by the blockading efforts of the Union's wooden warships. (Courtesy of the Naval History and Heritage Command, Photo Archives.)

The USS *Congress*, a sailing frigate built in 1841, was an important part of the Atlantic Blockading Squadron, anchoring off Newport News with orders to bottle up Hampton Roads and deny Virginia that avenue of trade. When the CSS *Virginia* appeared on March 8, 1862, the *Congress* was the first to be attacked. Indicative of how the Civil War divided not only states but also families, McKean Buchanan was paymaster onboard the *Congress*; his younger brother Franklin Buchanan was commander of the *Virginia*. (Courtesy of the Naval History and Heritage Command, Photo Archives.)

The *Congress* was no march for the smaller but far more powerful ironclad, her solid shot merely bouncing off the *Virginia*'s sides. The *Congress* ran aground and was relentlessly attacked by the foe. Losing 120 men, including her commander, Lt. Joseph B. Smith, and soon ablaze and unable to resist, the *Congress* hoisted the surrender flag. The flames eventually set off the *Congress*'s magazine, sending the frigate to the bottom. (Courtesy of the Naval History and Heritage Command, Photo Archives.)

The next victim for the ironclad *Virginia* was the USS *Cumberland*, a 50-gun frigate launched in 1842. One of the largest and most powerful ships in the Union navy, she had served as flagship to various squadrons. In April 1861, she was at the Gosport Navy Yard but was fortunate to escape destruction when towed out of harm's way. (Courtesy of the Naval History and Heritage Command, Photo Archives.)

Like the *Congress*, the USS *Cumberland* was back in Hampton Roads on blockade duty with a complement of 400 officers and men. Completing her devastating attack on the *Congress*, the *Virginia* turned her attention to the *Cumberland*, ramming the frigate and sending her to the bottom, killing many on board. To observers on the late afternoon on March 8, 1862, the destruction of two large and powerful ships meant a significant change in naval warfare. It was now a new age, with armored ships clearly having the advantage over the older wooden sailing vessels. (Courtesy of the Naval History and Heritage Command, Photo Archives.)

Keenly aware of the Confederacy's conversion of the Merrimack to the ironclad Virginia, the Union began its own efforts to build an ironclad in hopes of combating and destroying the Virginia and thus maintaining its blockade of Hampton Roads. But rather than creating another ironclad like the Virginia, the North created a truly revolutionary vessel: an iron ship with a revolving turret rather than the traditional broadside alignment of guns. The invention of the brilliant John Ericsson from the USS Princeton explosion (see pages 23–25), the USS Monitor, built in just over 100 days, arrived almost providentially in Hampton Roads on the night of March 8, 1862, guided to a moorage by the light coming from the still-burning USS Congress. (Courtesy of the Naval History and Heritage Command, Photo Archives.)

On the following morning, March 9, 1862, the two ironclads began their slow and rather awkward battle ballet, each inflicting relatively little damage on the other. The vessels, designed principally for their firepower and not as agile sailors, fought for four hours, often at very close range. A shell exploded at the *Monitor's* pilothouse, temporarily blinding the commanding officer, Lt. John Worden, and the Union ironclad briefly withdrew to assess the damage. The *Virginia*, believing the Union vessel was defeated and had surrendered, steamed back to Norfolk declaring victory. But then the *Monitor* returned and, seeing the *Virginia* leaving, assumed she had won the battle. The Battle of Hampton Roads was thus technically a draw. But since the *Virginia* did not return and the Union blockade of Hampton Roads remained, it was a Northern victory. (Courtesy of the Naval History and Heritage Command, Photo Archives.)

Neither of these technical marvels survived the year. The *Virginia* drew too much water for service on the James River and was far too unstable for any activity in open water. With Northern troops now moving to retake Norfolk and the Navy yard, the decision was made to strip her of everything useful and load her with explosives. On May 11, 1862, she was run up on Craney Island at the mouth of the Elizabeth River and blown up. (Courtesy of the Naval History and Heritage Command, Photo Archives.)

The Union navy decided that with Hampton Roads secure, the *Monitor* would be of greater value with the blockading efforts farther south on the Atlantic coast. Under tow by the USS *Rhode Island*—an indication that she was far from being a seaworthy vessel—she was lost in a storm off Cape Hatteras, North Carolina, on December 31, 1862. Most of her 62 sailors were saved by lifeboats from her consort, but 16 men were lost. Discovered in the 1970s, the *Monitor's* turret and other artifacts were recovered and are now undergoing conservation at The Mariners' Museum in Newport News. (Courtesy of the Naval History and Heritage Command, Photo Archives.)

The historic Battle of Hampton Roads forever changed naval warfare. But the Civil War saw hundreds more skirmishes in the many rivers and tributaries that feed the Chesapeake Bay. The James River connected the Confederate capital of Richmond to the Bay and the Atlantic. It is thus not surprising that the river saw numerous engagements of small, shallow-draft gunboats. The sidewheeler ferry *Ethan Allen* was converted by the Navy and named the USS *Commodore Barney* for the commander in the War of 1812 (see page 81). (Courtesy of the Naval History and Heritage Command, Photo Archives.)

Gunboats like the *Commodore Barney* were susceptible to Confederate shore batteries and prey to electrically activated mines, then called torpedoes. While on the upper reaches of the James River on August 4, 1863, a torpedo exploded under her, sending 20 sailors into the water and killing two. She was repaired and continued to see service for the remainder of the war. Many other vessels up and down the James River suffered similar fates, and many were left as shipwrecks. (Courtesy of the Naval History and Heritage Command, Photo Archives.)

Nations with inferior naval forces often resort to different types of weaponry, and the Confederacy was no exception. As seen here, it used ironclads and electric underwater mines. Another very successful tool was commerce-raiders, a relatively small but effective group of ships that, acting independently, attacked hundreds of Union commercial vessels around the world. The purpose was to force the North to remove ships from blockade duty in order to stop the raiders. Built overseas, the first foreign-built commerce-raider of the Civil War left Liverpool in the spring of 1862 for the Bahamas and was there commissioned the CSS *Florida*. Though Confederate commerce-raiders sailed the open seas, the *Florida* would ultimately end her life as a shipwreck in the Chesapeake Bay. (Courtesy of the Naval History and Heritage Command, Photo Archives.)

The CSS *Florida* captured or destroyed Union merchant vessels off the East Coast, in the West Indies, and in the open Atlantic. Here she is shown taking on the Union merchant ship *Jacob Bell* on February 12, 1863. She would take 37 prizes before arriving at Bahia, Brazil, on October 4, 1864. (Courtesy of the Naval History and Heritage Command, Photo Archives.)

At Bahia, with much of the *Florida's* crew ashore, the USS *Wachusett* slipped in and successfully seized the *Florida*. Ignoring diplomatic protests from the Brazilian government, the *Florida* was towed to Hampton Roads as a prize of war. The Brazilian protests continued, and the *Wachusett's* captain, Napoleon Collins, was court-martialed and found guilty of violating Brazilian territorial rights. However, Collins's conviction was overturned by Secretary of the Navy Gideon Welles, and Collins was subsequently promoted. (Courtesy of the Naval History and Heritage Command, Photo Archives.)

The captured *Florida* developed serious leaks while under tow, and on November 28, 1864, she was rammed by a troop ferry while anchored at Newport News. She sank despite efforts to keep her afloat. This might have been the end of the story, but the circumstances around her sinking were deemed mysterious. It was alleged that the US Navy allowed the *Florida* to sink in order to prevent her from being returned to Brazil—as was part of the court order—and thus likely resuming commerce-raiding activities for the Confederacy. This illustration is from *Leslie's Weekly* of December 24, 1864. (Courtesy of Hampton Roads Naval Museum.)

Four

STORMS

Despite the Chesapeake Bay being an estuary and theoretically more placid and safe than the open sea, it is not without its storms, and some of them are very significant and destructive. Those who live on or close to the Bay know how thunderstorms arrive quickly and unexpectedly. Nor'easters, in both warm weather and in winter, are also not that rare on the Chesapeake. Finally, full-fledged hurricanes are sadly not that unusual and can hit with incredible fury and destruction. Other types of dangerous weather in the Chesapeake include blizzards, hailstorms, and gales of all sizes and strengths.

In the days before accurate weather forecasts, sudden changes in the weather posed a serious threat to every sailor no matter what vessel he sailed and where in the Bay he was. Indeed, in the summer of 1608, one of the first Europeans in the Chesapeake wrote of his experience there with inclement weather. With a crew of 14, the famous captain John Smith set out in a small open shallop to explore the Chesapeake Bay up to the Patapsco River. Amongst many other dangers he and his men faced were storms that came up unexpectedly and with great ferocity. On June 4, 1608, Smith wrote: "with great danger we escaped the unmerciful raging of that ocean-like water. . . . We discovered the winde and the waters so much increased with thunder, lightning and rain that our mast and saile blew overboard, and such mighty waves overracked us in that small barge that with great labour we kept her from sinkimg by freeing out the water."

As one modern scholar, David Healey, has written, "When the weather is good in the Chesapeake, it's some of the best in the world. But the Chesapeake can raise a tempest on occasion." Many sailors over the centuries have come to realize and accept this truism.

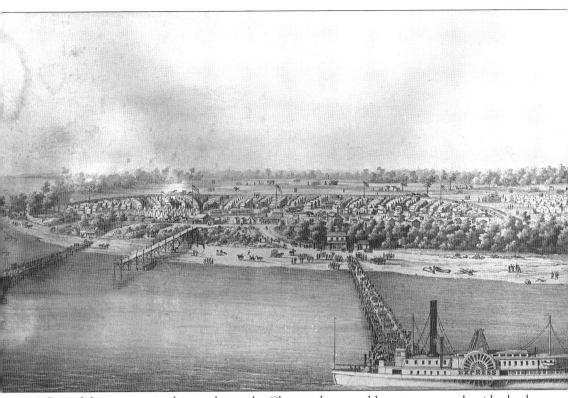

One of the most tragic shipwrecks on the Chesapeake caused by a storm was the sidewheeler *Express*, built in 1841 and operated by the Baltimore & Philadelphia Steamboat Company in the 1850s. Chartered by the US Army's Quartermaster Department for service during the Civil War, she ferried troops up and down the Chesapeake and its tributaries. Here, the *Express* is shown disembarking troops at Newport News. She returned to merchant service following the war, joining the Potomac Transportation Line operating out of Baltimore. In 1873, she was rebuilt with an extended hull. (Courtesy of The Mariners' Museum and Park.)

When the *Express* left Baltimore for the Potomac River and Washington, DC, with freight, a crew of 21, and 9 passengers, no one suspected that the steamer would be met by the "Gale of 1878," a storm of hurricane strength. In the early morning of October 23, the *Express* met the storm's full force; seas reached heights that dwarfed the steamer and tossed her relentlessly. The gale then tore off her saloon deck, including the lifeboat, and the sidewheeler broke up. Of those onboard the *Express*, only 15 survived. Capt. James T. Barker was later noted to have done all he could for the ship and passengers. He survived, but his young son did not. (Courtesy of the Library of Virginia.)

Not unlike the tragic collision that killed six midshipmen and six sailors in 1907 off Norfolk, another tragedy for the Navy occurred on the night of May 31, 1948, again at Norfolk and again with personnel returning from shore leave. A 50-foot Navy launch like this one and attached to the carrier USS Kearsarge in Hampton Roads was filled with returning crewmen on a Memorial Day liberty about 10:45 p.m. Nobody anticipated anything out of the ordinary on the two-mile trip between Norfolk and the ship when a fast-moving storm with high winds, rough seas, and a heavy current struck. The launch was a short distance from the carrier when she overturned in the storm. Few had on life vests, and while most swam to the ship's gangway and safety, 22 sailors and Marines drowned, their bodies swept away by the current. The subsequent report noted that the launch was badly overloaded, likely because it was the last one returning to the ship that evening. (Courtesy of the Naval History and Heritage Command, Photo Archives.)

No other weather-related sinking in the Chesapeake Bay—at least in modern times—was more significant than that of the *Levin J. Marvel* on August 12, 1955. Her tragic fate, taking the lives of 14 people, including children, became a front-page story up and down the East Coast. Built in 1891 as a three-masted, 125-foot cargo schooner, she spent nearly 60 years hauling bulk cargo. Never a sleek-lined, speedy schooner, her age plus wear and tear made her a poor sailor and a vessel near the end of her usefulness. (Courtesy of The Mariners' Museum and Park.)

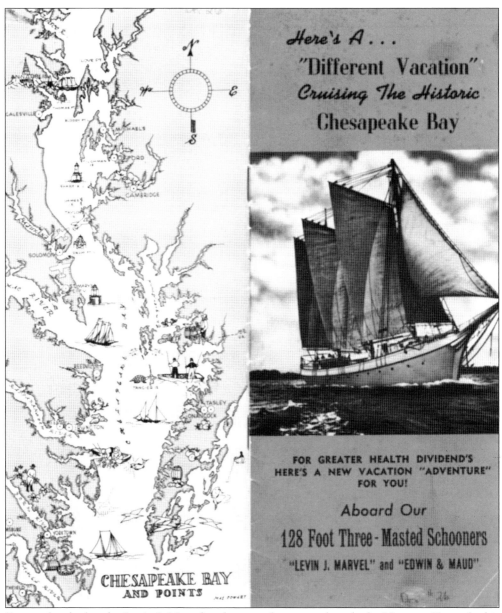

Despite her looks, the *Levin J. Marvel* and a sister boat were bought by Herman Knust for his Chesapeake Bay Vacation Cruises, beginning what was soon called the "Dude Cruise" industry on the Bay. Knust gutted the boat and added 17 staterooms with running water, electric lights, a galley and dining room, and a lounge. The one-week cruises afforded passengers the opportunity to experience sailing and working the schooner, not unlike dude ranches in the West. In 1946, the *Levin J. Marvel* even appeared in *Life* magazine when she became the biggest vessel to transit the 1,300-mile Intracoastal Waterway from Baltimore to Miami, although the voyage was not without numerous problems. (Courtesy of the Chesapeake Bay Maritime Museum, gift of Carl B. Bauer.)

In 1954, John Meckling bought the *Levin J. Marvel*, then needing major renovations. With little maritime or navigational experience, Meckling made a few improvements, then advertised for another sailing season. The *Levin J. Marvel* left Annapolis on August 8, 1955, for a six-day pleasure cruise with 23 passengers and 4 crewmen aboard. Meanwhile, 500 miles away, Hurricane Connie was nearing the East Coast. Returning to Annapolis, Meckling found the winds increasing to gale and then hurricane strength. Though he tried to reach safety south of Annapolis, waves came over the deck, and the hull quickly took on water. The death knell came when the schooner swung broadside to the waves. She capsized and split apart, and 14 people died. Meckling was found guilty of negligence and exposing passengers to danger, but he was acquitted of manslaughter and given a year's suspended sentence and probation. The tragedy did have one positive result: the Coast Guard was authorized to regularly inspect all commercial vessels that carried more than six passengers. (Courtesy of The Mariners' Museum and Park.)

Severe cold and ice in the Chesapeake can prove deadly. Tragedy struck the 50-foot *Hayruss IV*, which belonged to popular fisherman Garland Phillips from Tilghman Island, Maryland. The *Hayruss IV* went down in about 60 feet of icy water on February 9, 1979. Adding to the tragedy, four other fishermen on the boat, aged between 20 and 64 and all members of the same family, also died. All the bodies were fortunately recovered. Here, searchers off Tilghman Island send divers into the frigid waters to recover the *Hayruss IV*. (Courtesy of Capt. W.R. "Butch" Schuler [retired], Maryland Natural Resources Police.)

Towns up and down the Chesapeake Bay have memorials to residents who died on the Bay. This memorial lists 28 of the 33 watermen from Tilghman Island lost between 1891 and 1979. Another memorial was added to include nine more Tilghman Islanders who died between 1980 and 2015. (Author's collection.)

Five

ABANDONMENT

The final category of shipwrecks in the Chesapeake Bay is somewhat self-inflicted ones. Abandonment (usually by scuttling) has been very widely practiced over the centuries and throughout the world. Generally speaking, owners will deliberately sink their vessels—usually accomplished by letting water into the hull—in backwaters or other rarely used places. Abandonments also result when vessels sink and there are no resources to raise and salvage them. No one will ever know how many vessels of various sizes, types, and functions were abandoned in and around the Chesapeake Bay since the 17th century and the arrival of the first Europeans. But there is no area within the Bay and its tributaries that has not been the venue for an abandoned vessel of some type or size.

The reasons behind abandonments are many and diverse—a ship or boat may have lost its ability to compete, whether for economic reasons or perhaps because technology outpaced it. Owners might realize that it is too expensive to keep the vessel in operating, much less competitive, condition, and as such the boats simply become redundant and are abandoned. Purposeful abandonment of an old, no longer viable vessel might be done to restrict a certain part of a waterway, harbor, or channel. Ships of all types and sizes are also scuttled to create artificial reefs for divers or to help marine ecology. Abandoned ships are also used to help change the flow of a channel or river. Ships have also been purposely scuttled in order to prevent being captured by an enemy force, as seen with Joshua Barney's flotilla in the War of 1812 and the CSS *Virginia* in 1862.

While it is safe to assume that the vast majority of abandoned vessels are done so merely to get rid of them, there are very well-orchestrated and expensive efforts at purposely scuttling ships, like at Mallows Bay on the Potomac River or in the lower Chesapeake, where military ships were sunk after being bombarded as target vessels for gunnery practice.

One of the most famous examples on the Chesapeake Bay of a ship being purposely destroyed came during the run-up to the American Revolution. Amidst Colonial unrest and resistance to British taxes, a situation arose in Annapolis that was reminiscent of what happened in the Boston Tea Party of late 1773. The modest merchant brig *Peggy Stewart*, co-owned by Annapolitan Anthony Stewart and named for his daughter, was returning home carrying tea, the imported commodity that was especially enflaming many American patriots determined to boycott it. On October 19, 1774, angry citizens—showing their determination to resist what to them was British tyranny—forced the brig's owners to burn the *Peggy Stewart*. The remnants of the brig now rest in the reclaimed land under Luce Hall at the US Naval Academy. (Courtesy of the Maryland State Archives.)

The USS *Texas*, America's first true battleship, was launched on June 28, 1892, and gained great fame during the Spanish-American War as part of the force that defeated the Spanish fleet on July 3, 1898, off Santiago de Cuba, effectively ending the war and Spain's presence in Cuba. Regarded as obsolete a dozen years later as the global naval arms race intensified, she was renamed the USS *San Marcos* in February 1911, thus freeing up the name for the new and larger dreadnought USS *Texas* (BB-35). (Courtesy of the Naval History and Heritage Command, Photo Archives.)

The USS *San Marcos* would have a very short life. Barely a month after being renamed, she was towed up the Chesapeake Bay and anchored off Tangier Island, Virginia. The redundant warship was used as a target for both surface and aerial bombardment. This image shows the *San Marcos* before she was first fired upon, with canvas hoisted to help with aiming in the target exercises. (Courtesy of the Naval History and Heritage Command, Photo Archives.)

The new and powerful USS *New Hampshire* (BB-25) began in March 1911 what would be an intense series of bombardment target practices against the old *San Marcos*. (Courtesy of the Naval History and Heritage Command, Photo Archives.)

As this image shows, the *San Marcos* received incredible devastation as a target. She would remain off Tangier Island through World War II, when she was finally declared a navigation hazard. The US Navy planted explosives in January 1959 to drive the hulk into the mud, where she remains today. (Courtesy of the Naval History and Heritage Command, Photo Archives.)

Probably one of the more fascinating examples of scuttled ships in the Chesapeake Bay watershed is the famous Mallows Bay Ghost Fleet. Located in Charles County, Maryland, about 30 miles down the Potomac River from Washington, DC, Mallows Bay is one of the largest boat graveyards in the world. Here, about 230 vessels have been purposely sunk. (Courtesy of the Calvert Marine Museum, Fred Tilp Collection.)

In order to supply American forces in Europe during World War I, more than 100 wooden steamships were speedily and uniformly constructed of inferior material. But the war's short duration for the United States, cost overruns, and incredible mismanagement resulted in only about a tenth of the boats ever being completed. None of them made it to Europe. Being almost immediately obsolete, they were towed to Mallows Bay and burned on November 5, 1925. (Courtesy of the Calvert Marine Museum, Fred Tilp Collection.)

In addition to the vessels purposely burned there, many others of all types were taken to Mallows Bay. Many, if not most, were towed there without any formal permission and simply left, including the ferry *Accomac* (see page 18), schooners, and a menhaden fishing boat. Efforts to salvage and clean up Mallows Bay have been made, but in the early 1990s, the State of Maryland began a systematic study of the Bay's historic maritime resources. This led in 2015 to Mallows Bay being listed as an archaeological, ecological, and historic district in the National Register of Historic Places. In 2019, Mallows Bay was designated a national marine sanctuary by the National Oceanic and Atmospheric Administration. (Courtesy of Jayson Kowinsky, www.fossilguy.com.)

While most of the vessels in Mallows Bay are below the waterline, some can still be seen from the shoreline. (Author's collection.)

The foremost authority on Mallows Bay and indeed on the shipwreck history of the Chesapeake, Dr. Donald Shomette, wrote, "The shipwrecks of Mallows Bay have created a synthetic environment that . . . counteracts the pollution of the Potomac's water, filtering it and providing habitat and food to a wide range of life forms. In the process, each vessel has become a mini-ecosystem. Mallows Bay has again blossomed with biodiversity." (Courtesy of Jayson Kowinsky, www.fossilguy.com.)

One of the most beautiful and recognizable four-masted commercial schooners to sail the waters of the Chesapeake, the *Purnell T. White*, was built in 1917 on the Nanticoke River at Sharptown, Maryland, only a few miles from the Delaware state line—an indication of just how far inland the Bay's commercial and shipbuilding influence extends. On February 7, 1934, some 200 miles off Cape Fear, North Carolina, with her sails shredded by a freezing gale, ice forming on her deck, and water filling her hold, she sent a distress signal. The following day, the Coast Guard cutter *Mendota* arrived. The storm was so great that four of the seven crewmen on the *Purnell T. White* were lost. The dismasted schooner remained afloat, a testament to her craftsmanship, and was brought into Norfolk, salvaged, and taken to Baltimore to be converted into a barge. (Photograph by John R. Conley; courtesy of The Mariners' Museum and Park.)

As anyone who has experience with boats—especially wooden ones—knows, time and the elements combine to produce a lethal result. The owners waited too long, and the once-beautiful *Purnell T. White* rotted at Baltimore's Locust Point. (Courtesy of the Chesapeake Bay Maritime Museum, Robert H. Burgess Collection.)

Plans to dredge the area for a new terminal resulted in the hulk being refloated and towed to Hawkins Point at Curtis Bay, on the south side of the Patapsco River, a favorite place for abandoned vessels of all types until the past few years. The once-proud *Purnell T. White's* remains could be seen as late as the 1980s. (Courtesy of The Mariners' Museum and Park.)

One of the strangest stories dealing with a Chesapeake Bay shipwreck is that of the submarine S-49. Launched in 1921 with a crew of 52 officers and men, the boat was too late to participate in World War I. She was subsequently used in torpedo research out of New London, Connecticut. On April 20, 1926, two batteries exploded and injured a dozen crewmen, four of whom later died from their injuries. Laid up at League Island, Pennsylvania, she was stricken from the Navy in March 1931 in accordance with the London Naval Treaty. Then the boat went from a submarine research vessel to a traveling attraction run by a raconteur to making US Supreme Court history to naval research again and finally to foundering. (Courtesy of the Naval History and Heritage Command, Photo Archives.)

Bought by "Captain" Francis J. Chrestensen in late 1931, the S-49 became a touring floating attraction up and down the East Coast and the Great Lakes. (Courtesy of Ric Hedman.)

This photograph of the S-49 was taken while she was on show at the Great Lakes Exposition in Cleveland, Ohio, in 1936, obviously thrilling crowds. (Courtesy of the Naval History and Heritage Command, Photo Archives.)

Here she is "on the hard" at Point-O-Pines in Revere, Massachusetts, about 1935. In 1940, Chrestensen was accused of violating a New York City ordnance against distributing advertising handbills. In a case that went to the US Supreme Court, the ruling went against Chrestensen, and it became the first major case to address the limits of commercial speech. The Navy reacquired the S-49 for experimental work at Solomons, Maryland, but while being towed there, the submarine foundered off Point Patience in the Patuxent River on December 16, 1942, and sank in about 130 feet of water. (Courtesy of Ric Hedman.)

With the rare distinction of having served in the Army, Navy, Air Force, and Coast Guard, the *American Mariner* was launched in December 1941 and became a cadet training vessel for the US Coast Guard. She was loaded with the most high-tech equipment to detect missiles before they re-entered the earth's atmosphere and was used for NASA's Project Mercury. The *American Mariner* was subsequently sent in October 1963 to the Air Force and then to the Navy. (Courtesy of the Naval History and Heritage Command, Photo Archives.)

By October 1966, the *American Mariner* had outlived her usefulness. Subsequently, she was scuttled halfway between Point Lookout and Smith Island. Settling upright in about 20 feet, the hulk was used for target practice by naval aviators flying out of Naval Air Station Patuxent River, Maryland, until about 1972. She is still visible in the Bay. (Courtesy of Michael A. Smolek.)

The USS *McKeever Brothers* (SP-683), shown here in Philadelphia in 1918, was originally a menhaden fishing trawler built in Noank, Connecticut, in 1911, and owned by brothers Steven and Edward McKeever. During World War I, with a crew of 22, she served as a patrol boat and minesweeper in the Delaware River and the Chesapeake Bay. She was sold in July 1919 and returned to her original trawler functions. (Courtesy of the Naval History and Heritage Command, Photo Archives.)

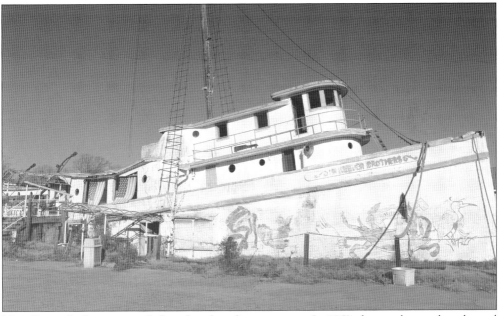

Not all vessels that are scuttled or abandoned are on water. In 1969, the trawler was bought and converted into a floating restaurant in Seaford, Delaware, named the Flagship Nanticoke Queen, and advertised as serving "fine steaks, seafood and cocktails in a setting enhanced by mellowed old wooden beams and planking, brass fittings and soft music [with] a 'Red Carpet' setting!" The restaurant eventually closed around 2005. She still sits deteriorating on Route 13 near the Nanticoke River in Seaford. (Author's collection.)

Following World War II, the Virginia Ferry Corporation, which ran the route between the lower Eastern Shore and Norfolk, moved its terminal from Cape Charles to Kiptopeke, Virginia. But the new terminal needed protection from the ravages of weather. The answer came from concrete ships. Built in 1943 in Tampa, the concrete ships were named for pioneers in the use of concrete. Many were used as store ships in the Pacific and European theaters during the war. This is the *Arthur Newell Talbot*. (Courtesy of The Mariners' Museum and Park.)

Beginning in 1948, nine concrete ships were partially sunk in two rows running parallel with the shoreline at Kiptopeke, thus forming an ideal ferry breakwater. (Courtesy of The Mariners' Museum and Park.)

Although the Chesapeake Bay Bridge-Tunnel effectively ended ferry service in 1964, the ships continue to protect Kiptopeke Beach, providing now homes for various species of wildlife. (Courtesy of the Virginia Department of Conservation and Recreation.)

The Chesapeake Bay has certainly seen its share of shipwrecks—no matter the cause—since the early 17th century and the arrival of the first Europeans. This image of Curtis Bay—one of several graveyards in the Chesapeake that has been used for scuttled and abandoned ships—shows the forlorn beauty of a vessel's last years. (Courtesy of The Mariners' Museum and Park.)

Bibliography

Brown, Alexander Crosby. *Steam Packets of the Chesapeake: A History of the Old Bay Line since 1840.* Centreville, MD: Tidewater Publishers, 1961.

Burgess, Robert H., and H. Graham Wood. *Steamboats out of Baltimore.* Cambridge, MD: Tidewater Publishers, 1968.

Dictionary of American Naval Fighting Ships. Washington, DC: Naval Heritage Center, 1959–1981.

Elliott, Richard V. *Last of the Steamboats: Saga of the Wilson Line.* Cambridge, MD: Tidewater Publishers, 1970.

Gaines, W. Craig. *Encyclopedia of Civil War Shipwrecks.* Baton Rouge, LA: Louisiana State University Press, 2008.

Gentile, Gary. *Shipwrecks of Virginia.* Philadelphia, PA: Gary Gentile Productions, 1992.

———. *Shipwrecks of the Chesapeake Bay and Maryland Waters.* Jim Thorpe, PA: Gary Gentile Publications, 2013.

Healey, David. *Great Storms of the Chesapeake.* Charleston, SC: The History Press, 2012.

Holly, David C. *Chesapeake Steamboats: Vanished Fleet.* Centreville, MD: Tidewater Publishers, 1994.

———. *Steamboat on the Chesapeake:* Emma Giles *and the Tolchester Line.* Centreville, MD: Tidewater Publishers, 1987.

———. *Tidewater by Steamboat: A Saga of the Chesapeake.* Baltimore, MD: Johns Hopkins University Press, 1991.

Jones, Harry, and Timothy Jones. *Night Boat on the Potomac: A History of Norfolk and Washington Steamboat Company.* Warwick, RI: Steamship Historical Society, 1996.

Keith, Robert C. *Baltimore Harbor: A Pictorial History.* 3rd ed. Baltimore, MD: Johns Hopkins University Press, 2005.

Lonsdale, Adrian, and H.R. Kaplan. *A Guide to Sunken Ships in American Waters.* Arlington, VA: Compass Publications, 1964.

Shomette, Donald G. *Flotilla: Battle for the Patuxent.* Solomons, MD: Calvert Marine Museum Press, 1981.

———. *Shipwrecks of the Chesapeake: Maritime Disasters on Chesapeake Bay and Its Tributaries, 1608–1978.* Centreville, MD: Tidewater Publishers, 1982.

———. *Shipwrecks of the Civil War: The Encyclopedia of Union and Confederate Naval Losses.* Washington, D.C.: Donie, 1973.

DISCOVER THOUSANDS OF LOCAL HISTORY BOOKS
FEATURING MILLIONS OF VINTAGE IMAGES

Arcadia Publishing, the leading local history publisher in the United States, is committed to making history accessible and meaningful through publishing books that celebrate and preserve the heritage of America's people and places.

Find more books like this at
www.arcadiapublishing.com

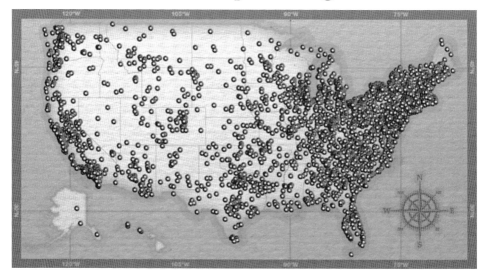

Search for your hometown history, your old stomping grounds, and even your favorite sports team.

Consistent with our mission to preserve history on a local level, this book was printed in South Carolina on American-made paper and manufactured entirely in the United States. Products carrying the accredited Forest Stewardship Council (FSC) label are printed on 100 percent FSC-certified paper.

MADE IN THE
USA